Mandal

DAYS OF MIRACLES

My name is:

Miracles happen when you thank with the Soul, which is eternal, and forgive with the heart, which has an end.
"Carolina Lasso R"

Lesson 1
Nothing I See Means Anything.
Nothing I see in this room [on this street, from this window, in this place] means anything.

Lesson 2
I have given everything I see all the meaning that it has for me.
I have given everything I see in this room [on this street, from this window, in this place] all the meaning that it has for me.

Lesson 3
I do not understand anything I see.
I do not understand anything I see in this room
[on this street, from this window, in this place].

Lesson 4
These thoughts do not mean anything.
These thoughts do not mean anything. They are like the things I see in this room [on this street, from this window, in this place].

Lesson 5
I am never upset for the reason I think.

Lesson 6
I am upset because I see something that is not there.

Lesson 7
I see only the past.

Lesson 8
My mind is preoccupied with past thoughts.

Lesson 9
I see nothing as it is now.

Lesson 10
My thoughts do not mean anything.

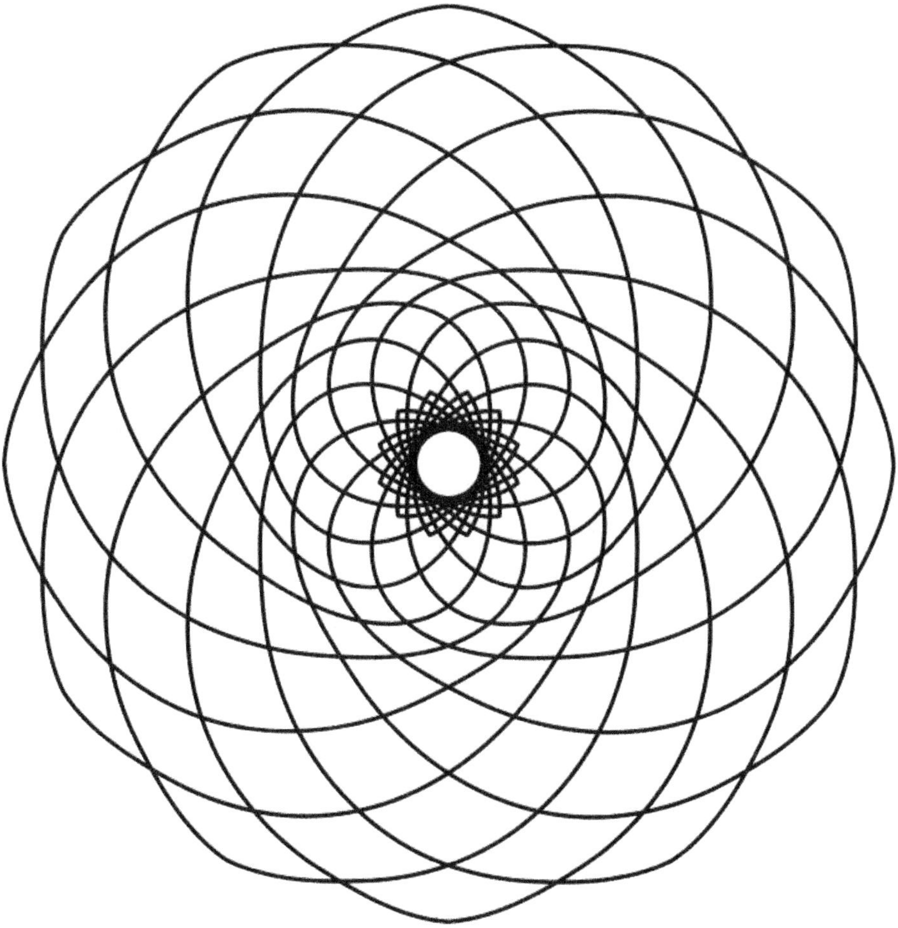

Lesson 11
My meaningless thoughts are showing me a meaningless world.

Lesson 12
I am upset because I see a meaningless world.

Lesson 13
A meaningless world engenders fear.

Lesson 14
God did not create a meaningless world.

Lesson 15
My thoughts are images that I have made.

Lesson 16
I have no neutral thoughts.

Lesson 17
I see no neutral things.

Lesson 18
I am not alone in experiencing the effects of my seeing.

Lesson 19
I am not alone in experiencing the effects of my thoughts.

Lesson 20
I am determined to see.

Lesson 21
I am determined to see things differently.

Lesson 22
What I see is a form of vengeance.

Lesson 23
I can escape from the world I see by giving up attack thoughts.

Lesson 24
I do not perceive my own best interests.

Lesson 25
I do not know what anything is for.

Lesson 26
My attack thoughts are attacking my invulnerability.

Lesson 27
Above all else I want to see.

Lesson 28
Above all else I want to see things differently.

Lesson 29
God is in everything I see.

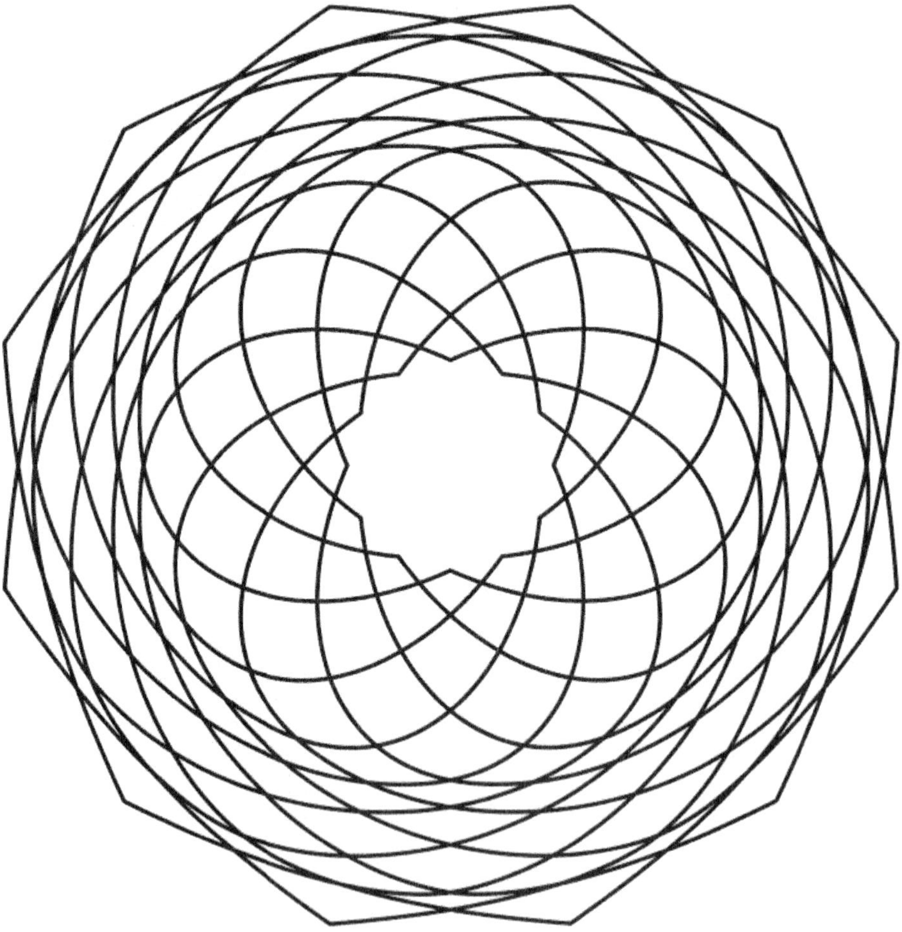

Lesson 30
God is in everything I see because God is in my mind.

Lesson 31
I am not the victim of the world I see.

Lesson 32
I have invented the world I see.

Lesson 33
There is another way of looking at the world.

Lesson 34
I could see peace instead of this.

Lesson 35
My mind is part of God's. I am very holy.

365 DAYS OF MIRACLES

Lesson 36
My holiness envelops everything I see.

365 DAYS OF MIRACLES

Lesson 37
My holiness blesses the world.

365 DAYS OF MIRACLES

Lesson 38
There is nothing my holiness cannot do.

Lesson 39
My holiness is my salvation.

365 DAYS OF MIRACLES

Lesson 40
I am blessed as a Son of God.

Lesson 41
God goes with me wherever I go.

365 DAYS OF MIRACLES

Lesson 42
God is my strength. Vision is His gift.

365 DAYS OF MIRACLES

Lesson 43
God is my Source. I cannot see apart from Him.

Lesson 44
God is the light in which I see.

Lesson 45
God is the Mind with which I think.

365 DAYS OF MIRACLES

Lesson 46
God is the Love in which I forgive.

365 DAYS OF MIRACLES

Lesson 47
God is the strength in which I trust.

365 DAYS OF MIRACLES

Lesson 48
There is nothing to fear.

365 DAYS OF MIRACLES

Lesson 49
God's Voice speaks to me all through the day.

365 DAYS OF MIRACLES

Lesson 50
I am sustained by the Love of God.

First Review - Lesson 51 - Review of Lessons 1 - 5
The review for today covers the following ideas:
1. (1) Nothing I see means anything. 2. (2) I have given what I see all the meaning it has for me. 3. (3) I do not understand anything I see. 4. (4) These thoughts do not mean anything. 5. (5) I am never upset for the reason I think.

First Review – Lesson 52 – Review of Lessons 6 – 10
Today's review covers these ideas:
1. (6) I am upset because I see what is not there. 2. (7) I see only the past. 3. (8) My mind is preoccupied with past thoughts. 4. (9) I see nothing as it is now. 5. (10) My thoughts do not mean anything.

365 DAYS OF MIRACLES

First Review – Lesson 53 – Review of Lessons 10 – 15
Today we will review the following: 1. (11) My meaningless thoughts are showing me a meaningless world. 2. (12) I am upset because I see a meaningless world. 3. (13) A meaningless world engenders fear. 4. (14) God did not create a meaningless world. 5. (15) My thoughts are images that I have made.

First Review – Lesson 54 – Review of Lessons 16 – 20
These are the review ideas for today: 1. (16) I have no neutral thoughts. 2. (17) I have no neutral thoughts. 3. (18) I am not alone in experiencing the effects of my seeing. 4. (19) I am not alone in experiencing the effects of my thoughts. 5. (20) I am determined to see.

365 DAYS OF MIRACLES

First Review - Lesson 55 - Review of Lessons 21 - 25
Today's review includes the following: 1. (21) I am determined to see things differently. 2. (22) What I see is a form of vengeance. 3. (23) I can escape from this world by giving up attack thoughts. 4. (24) I do not perceive my own best interests. 5. (25) I do not know what anything is for.

First Review – Lesson 56 – Review of Lessons 26 – 30
Our review for today covers the following: 1. (26) My attack thoughts are attacking my invulnerability. 2. (27) Above all else I want to see. 3. (28) Above all else I want to see differently. 4. (29) God is in everything I see. 5. (30) God is in everything I see because God is in my mind.

First Review - Lesson 57 - Review of Lessons 31 - 35
Today let us review these ideas: 1. (31) I am not the victim of the world I see. 2. (32) I have invented the world I see. 3. (33) There is another way of looking at the world. 4. (34) I could see peace instead of this. 5. (35) My mind is part of God's.

365 DAYS OF MIRACLES

First Review – Lesson 58 – Review of Lessons 36 – 40
These ideas are for review today: 1. (36) My holiness envelops everything I see. 2. (37) My holiness blesses the world. 3. (38) There is nothing my holiness cannot do. 4. (39) My holiness is my salvation. 5. (40) I am blessed as a Son of God.

365 DAYS OF MIRACLES

First Review – Lesson 59 – Review of Lessons 41 – 45
The following ideas are for review today: 1. (41) God goes with me wherever I go. 2. (42) God is my strength. Vision is His gift. 3. (43) God is my Source. 4. (44) God is the light in which I see. 5. (45) God is the Mind with which I think.

365 DAYS OF MIRACLES

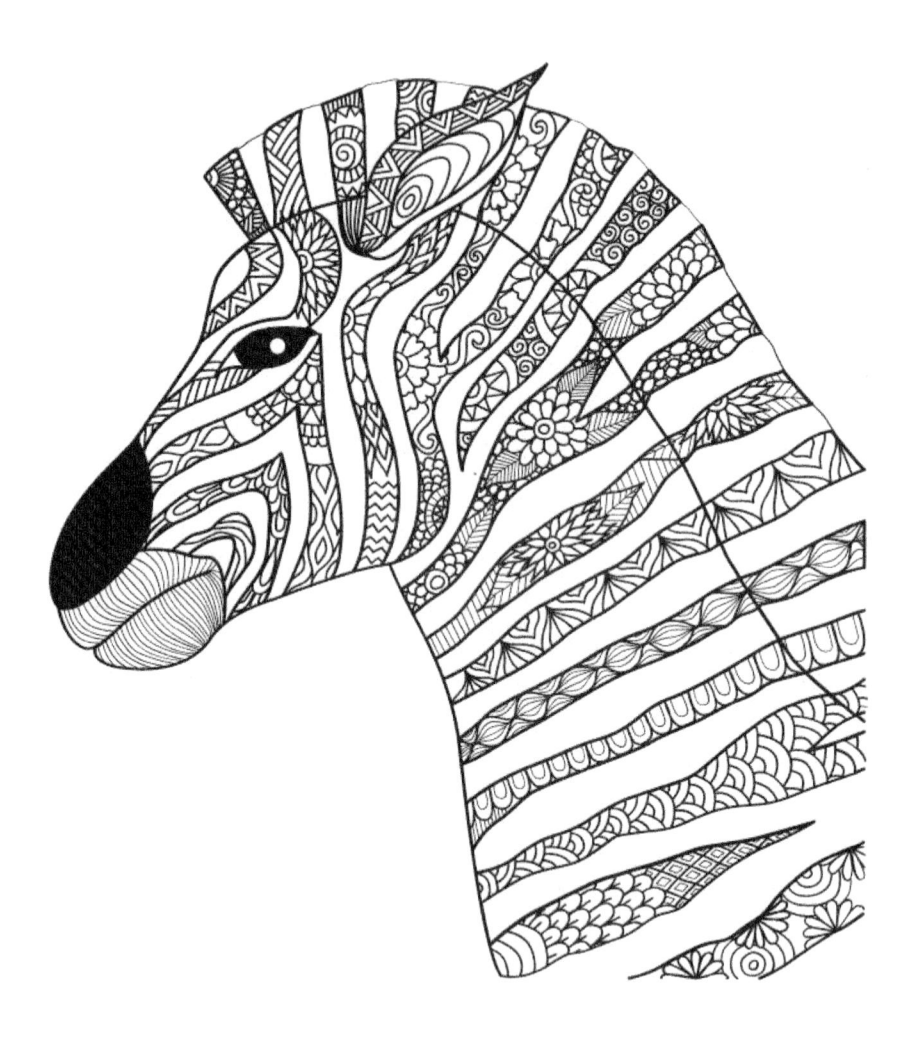

First Review - Lesson 60 - Review of Lessons 46 - 50
These ideas are for today's review: 1. (46) God is the Love in which I forgive. 2. (47) God is the strength in which I trust. 3. (48) There is nothing to fear. 4. (49) God's Voice speaks me all through the day. 5. (50) I am sustained by the Love of God.

365 DAYS OF MIRACLES

Lesson 61
I am the light of the world.

365 DAYS OF MIRACLES

Lesson 62
Forgiveness is my function as the light of the world.

Lesson 63
The light of the world brings peace
to every mind through my forgiveness.

365 DAYS OF MIRACLES

Lesson 64
Let me not forget my function.

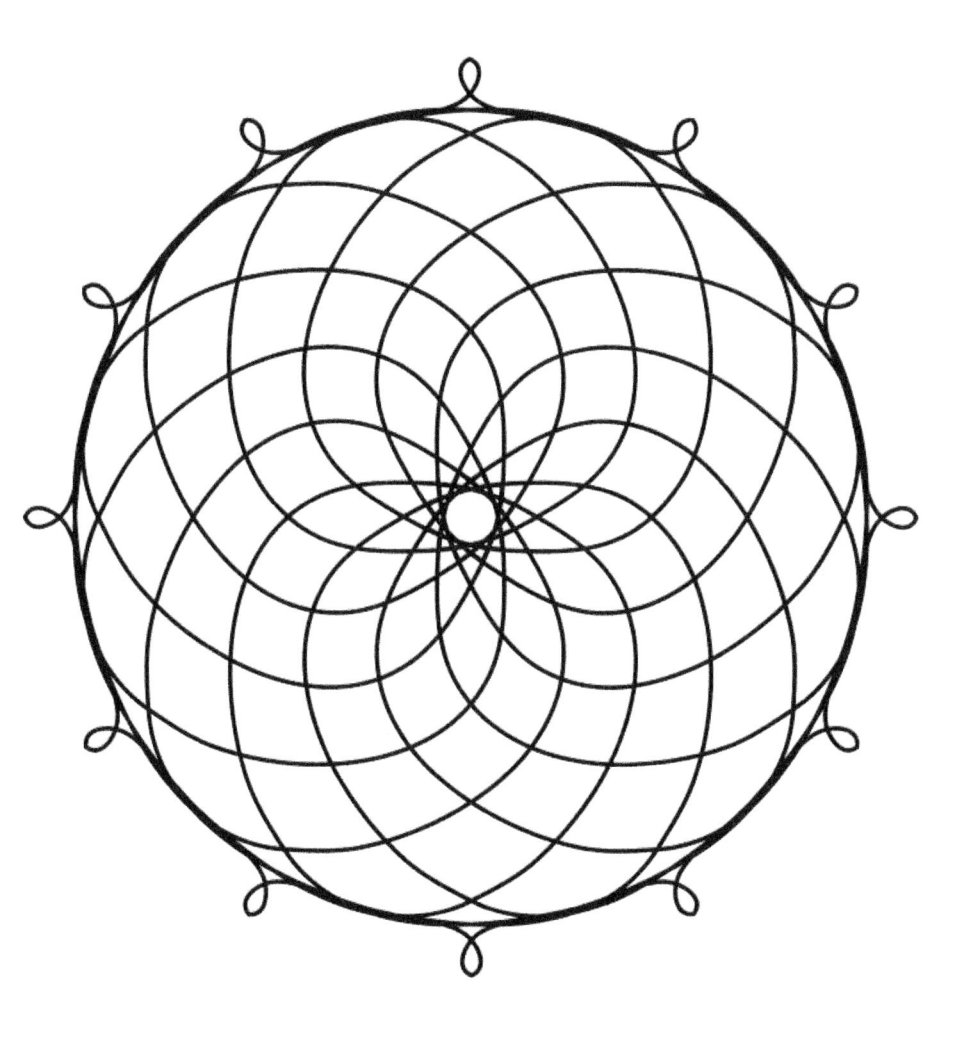

Lesson 65
My only function is the one God gave me.

Lesson 66
My happiness and my function are one.

Lesson 67
Love created me like itself.

Lesson 68
Love holds no grievances.

Lesson 69
My grievances hide the light of the world in me.

365 DAYS OF MIRACLES

Lesson 70
My salvation comes from me.

365 DAYS OF MIRACLES

Lesson 71
Only God's plan for salvation will work.

365 DAYS OF MIRACLES

Lesson 72
Holding grievances is an attack on God's plan for salvation.

Lesson 73
I will there be light.

365 DAYS OF MIRACLES

Lesson 74
There is no will but God's.

Lesson 75
The light has come.

365 DAYS OF MIRACLES

Lesson 76
I am under no laws but God's.

365 DAYS OF MIRACLES

Lesson 77
I am entitled to miracles.

365 DAYS OF MIRACLES

Lesson 78
Let miracles replace all grievances.

Lesson 79
Let me recognize the problem so it can be solved.

365 DAYS OF MIRACLES

Lesson 80
Let me recognize my problems have been solved.

Second Review – Lesson 81 – Review of Lessons 61 – 62
Our ideas for review today are: 1. (61) I am the light of the world. 2. (62) Forgiveness is my function as the light of the world.

365 DAYS OF MIRACLES

Second Review - Lesson 82 - Review of Lessons 63 - 64
We will review these ideas today: 1. (63) The light of the world brings peace to every mind through my forgiveness. 2. (64) Let me not forget my function.

Second Review – Lesson 83 – Review of Lessons 65 – 66
Today let us review these ideas: 1. (65) My only function is the one God gave me. 2. (66) My happiness and my function are one.

Second Review – Lesson 84 – Review of Lessons 67 – 68
These are the ideas for today's review: 1. (67) Love created me like itself. 2. (68) Love holds no grievances.

Second Review – Lesson 85 – Review of Lessons 69 – 70
Today's review will cover these ideas: 1. (69) My grievances hide the light of the world in me. 2. (70) My salvation comes from me.

Second Review - Lesson 86 - Review of Lessons 71 - 72
These ideas are for review today: 1. (71) Only God's plan for salvation will work. 2. (72) Holding grievances is an attack on God's plan for salvation.

Second Review – Lesson 87 – Review of Lessons 73 – 74
Our review today will cover these ideas: 1. (73) I will there be light. 2. (74) There is no will but God's.

365 DAYS OF MIRACLES

Second Review – Lesson 88 – Review of Lessons 75 – 76
Today we will review these ideas: 1. (75) The light has come.
2. (76) I am under no laws but God's.

Second Review - Lesson 89 - Review of Lessons 77 - 78
These are our review ideas for today: 1. (77) I am entitled to miracles. 2. (78) Let miracles replace all grievances.

365 DAYS OF MIRACLES

Second Review – Lesson 90 – Review of Lessons 79 – 80
For this review we will use these ideas: 1. (79) Let me recognize the problem so it can be solved. 2. (80) Let me recognize my problems have been solved.

365 DAYS OF MIRACLES

Lesson 91
Miracles are seen in light.

Lesson 92
Miracles are seen in light, and light and strength are one.

Lesson 93
Light and joy and peace abide in me.

365 DAYS OF MIRACLES

Lesson 94
I am as God created me.

365 DAYS OF MIRACLES

Lesson 95
I am one Self, united with my Creator.

365 DAYS OF MIRACLES

Lesson 96
Salvation comes from my one Self.

365 DAYS OF MIRACLES

Lesson 97
I am spirit.

365 DAYS OF MIRACLES

Lesson 98
I will accept my part in God's plan for salvation.

Lesson 99
Salvation is my only function here.

365 DAYS OF MIRACLES

Lesson 100
My part is essential to God's plan for salvation.

365 DAYS OF MIRACLES

Lesson 101
God's Will for me is perfect happiness.

365 DAYS OF MIRACLES

Lesson 102
I share God's Will for happiness for me.

Lesson 103
God, being Love, is also happiness.

365 DAYS OF MIRACLES

Lesson 104
I seek but what belongs to me in truth.

Lesson 105
God's peace and joy are mine.

365 DAYS OF MIRACLES

Lesson 106
Let me be still and listen to the truth.

365 DAYS OF MIRACLES

Lesson 107
Truth will correct all errors in my mind.

365 DAYS OF MIRACLES

Lesson 108
To give and to receive are one in truth.

365 DAYS OF MIRACLES

Lesson 109
I rest in God.

365 DAYS OF MIRACLES

Lesson 110
I am as God created me.

Third Review - Lesson 111 - Review of Lessons 91 - 92
For morning and evening review: 1. (91) Miracles are seen in light. 2. (92) Miracles are seen in light, and light and strength are one.

365 DAYS OF MIRACLES

Third Review – Lesson 112 – Review of Lessons 93 – 94
For morning and evening review: 1. (93) Light and joy and peace abide in me. 2. (94) I am as God created me.

Third Review – Lesson 113 – Review of Lessons 95 – 96
For morning and evening review: 1. (95) I am one Self, united with my Creator. 2. (96) Salvation comes from my one Self.

Third Review - Lesson 114 - Review of Lessons 97 - 98
For morning and evening review: 1. (97) I am spirit. I am the Son of God. 2. (98) I will accept my part in God's plan for salvation.

Third Review - Lesson 115 - Review of Lessons 99 - 100
For morning and evening review: 1. (99) Salvation is my only function here. 2. (100) My part is essential to God's plan for salvation.

Third Review – Lesson 116 – Review of Lessons 101 – 102
For morning and evening review: 1. (101) God's Will for me is perfect happiness. 2. (102) I share God's Will for happiness for me.

Third Review - Lesson 117 - Review of Lessons 103 - 104
For morning and evening review: 1. (103) God, being Love, is also happiness. 2. (104) I seek but what belongs to me in truth.

365 DAYS OF MIRACLES

Third Review – Lesson 118 – Review of Lessons 105 – 106
For morning and evening review: 1. (105) God's peace and joy are mine. 2. (106) Let me be still and listen to the truth.

Third Review – Lesson 119 – Review of Lessons 107 – 108
For morning and evening review: 1. (107) Truth will correct all errors in my mind. 2. (108) To give and to receive are one in truth.

Third Review - Lesson 120 - Review of Lessons 109 - 110
For morning and evening review: 1. (109) I rest in God.
2. (110) I am as God created me.

365 DAYS OF MIRACLES

Lesson 121
Forgiveness is the key to happiness.

365 DAYS OF MIRACLES

Lesson 122
Forgiveness offers everything I want.

365 DAYS OF MIRACLES

Lesson 123
I thank my Father for His gifts to me.

365 DAYS OF MIRACLES

Lesson 124
Let me remember I am one with God.

365 DAYS OF MIRACLES

Lesson 125
In quiet I receive God's Word today.

365 DAYS OF MIRACLES

Lesson 126
All that I give is given to myself.

365 DAYS OF MIRACLES

Lesson 127
There is no love but God's.

365 DAYS OF MIRACLES

Lesson 128
The world I see holds nothing that I want.

365 DAYS OF MIRACLES

Lesson 129
Beyond this world there is a world I want.

365 DAYS OF MIRACLES

Lesson 130
It is impossible to see two worlds.

365 DAYS OF MIRACLES

Lesson 131
No one can fail who seeks to reach the truth.

365 DAYS OF MIRACLES

Lesson 132
I loose the world from all I thought it was.

365 DAYS OF MIRACLES

Lesson 133
I will not value what is valueless.

365 DAYS OF MIRACLES

Lesson 134
Let me perceive forgiveness as it is.

Lesson 135
If I defend myself I am attacked.

365 DAYS OF MIRACLES

Lesson 136
Sickness is a defense against the truth.

Lesson 137

When I am healed I am not healed alone.

365 DAYS OF MIRACLES

Lesson 138
Heaven is the decision I must make.

365 DAYS OF MIRACLES

Lesson 139
I will accept Atonement for myself.

365 DAYS OF MIRACLES

Lesson 140
Only salvation can be said to cure.

Fourth Review - Lesson 141 - Review of Lessons 121-122
My mind holds only what I think with God.
(121) Forgiveness is the key to happiness.
(122) Forgiveness offers everything I want.

Fourth Review – Lesson 142 – Review of Lessons 123 –124
My mind holds only what I think with God.
(123) I thank my Father for His gifts to me.
(124) Let me remember I am one with God.

365 DAYS OF MIRACLES

Fourth Review - Lesson 143 - Review of Lessons 125 -126
My mind holds only what I think with God.
(125) In quiet I receive God's Word today.
(126) All that I give is given to myself.

Fourth Review – Lesson 144 – Review of Lessons 127 –128
My mind holds only what I think with God.
(127) There is no love but God's.
(128) The world I see holds nothing that I want.

365 DAYS OF MIRACLES

Fourth Review - Lesson 145 - Review of Lessons 129 -130
My mind holds only what I think with God.
(129) Beyond this world there is a world I want.
(130) It is impossible to see two worlds.

Fourth Review - Lesson 146 - Review of Lessons 131 -132
My mind holds only what I think with God.
(131) No one can fail who seeks to reach the truth.
(132) I loose the world from all I thought it was.

Fourth Review - Lesson 147 - Review of Lessons 133 -134
My mind holds only what I think with God.
(133) I will not value what is valueless.
(134) Let me perceive forgiveness as it is.

Fourth Review - Lesson 148 - Review of Lessons 135 -136
My mind holds only what I think with God.
(135) If I defend myself I am attacked.
(136) Sickness is a defense against the truth.

365 DAYS OF MIRACLES

Fourth Review - Lesson 149 - Review of Lessons 137 - 138
My mind holds only what I think with God.
(137) When I am healed I am not healed alone.
(138) Heaven is the decision I must make.

365 DAYS OF MIRACLES

Fourth Review – Lesson 150 – Review of Lessons 139 –140
My mind holds only what I think with God.
(139) I will accept Atonement for myself.
(140) Only salvation can be said to cure.

365 DAYS OF MIRACLES

Lesson 151
All things are echoes of the Voice for God.

365 DAYS OF MIRACLES

Lesson 152
The power of decision is my own.

365 DAYS OF MIRACLES

Lesson 153
In my defenselessness my safety lies.

365 DAYS OF MIRACLES

Lesson 154
I am among the ministers of God.

Lesson 155
I will step back and let Him lead the way.

Lesson 156
I walk with God in perfect holiness.

365 DAYS OF MIRACLES

Lesson 157
Into His Presence would I enter now.

365 DAYS OF MIRACLES

Lesson 158
Today I learn to give as I receive.

Lesson 159
I give the miracles I have received.

365 DAYS OF MIRACLES

Lesson 160
I am at home. Fear is the stranger here.

365 DAYS OF MIRACLES

Lesson 161
Give me your blessing, holy Son of God.

365 DAYS OF MIRACLES

Lesson 162
I am as God created me.

365 DAYS OF MIRACLES

Lesson 163
There is no death. The Son of God is free.

Lesson 164
Now are we one with Him Who is our Source.

Lesson 165
Let not my mind deny the Thought of God.

365 DAYS OF MIRACLES

Lesson 166
I am entrusted with the gifts of God.

365 DAYS OF MIRACLES

Lesson 167
There is one life, and that I share with God.

365 DAYS OF MIRACLES

Lesson 168
Your grace is given me. I claim it now.

Lesson 169
By grace I live. By grace I am released.

365 DAYS OF MIRACLES

Lesson 170
There is no cruelty in God and none in me.

Fifth Review – Lesson 171 – Review of Lessons 151 – 152
God is but Love, and therefore so am I.
1. (151) All things are echoes of the Voice for God.
2. (152) The power of decision is my own.

365 DAYS OF MIRACLES

Fifth Review – Lesson 172 – Review of Lessons 153 – 154
God is but Love, and therefore so am I.
1. (153) In my defenselessness my safety lies.
2. (154) I am among the ministers of God.

365 DAYS OF MIRACLES

Fifth Review – Lesson 173 – Review of Lessons 155 – 156
God is but Love, and therefore so am I.
1. (155) I will step back and let Him lead the way.
2. (156) I walk with God in perfect holiness.

Fifth Review – Lesson 174 – Review of Lessons 157 – 158
God is but Love, and therefore so am I.
1. (157) Into His Presence would I enter now.
2. (158) Today I learn to give as I receive.

Fifth Review – Lesson 175 – Review of Lessons 159 – 160
God is but Love, and therefore so am I.
1. (159) I give the miracles I have received.
2. (160) I am at home. Fear is the stranger here.

Fifth Review – Lesson 176 – Review of Lessons 161 – 162
God is but Love, and therefore so am I.
1. (161) Give me your blessing, holy Son of God.
2. (162) I am as God created me.

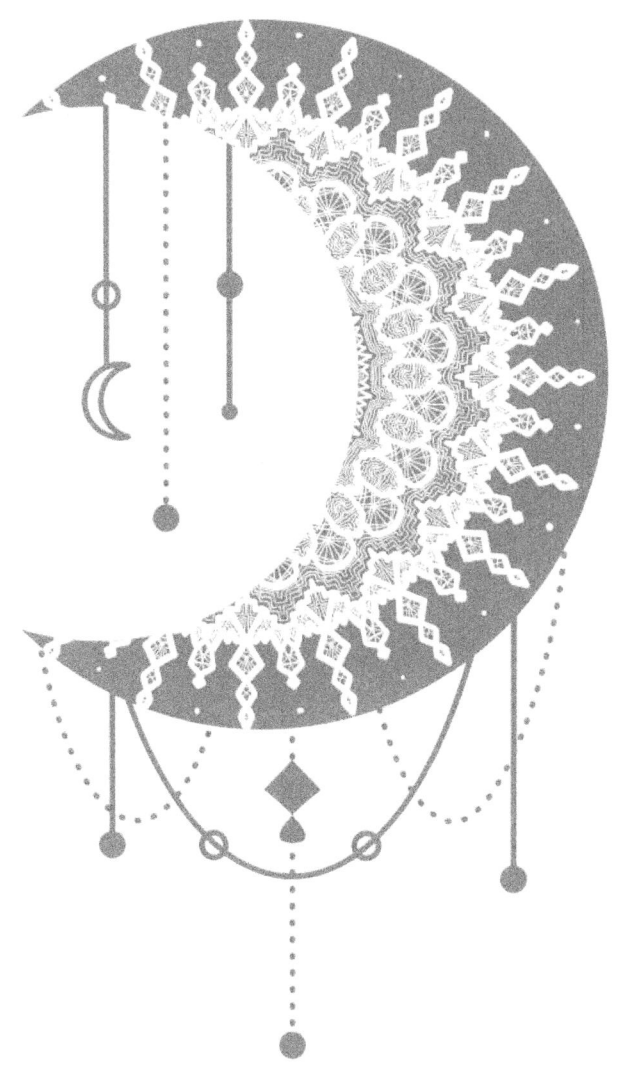

Fifth Review – Lesson 177 – Review of Lessons 163 – 164
God is but Love, and therefore so am I.
1. (163) There is no death. The Son of God is free.
2. (164) Now are we one with Him Who is our Source.

Fifth Review – Lesson 178 – Review of Lessons 165 - 166
God is but Love, and therefore so am I.
1. (165) Let not my mind deny the Thought of God.
2. (166) I am entrusted with the gifts of God.

Fifth Review – Lesson 179 – Review of Lessons 167 – 168
God is but Love, and therefore so am I.
1. (167) There is one life, and that I share with God.
2. (168) Your grace is given me. I claim it now.

365 DAYS OF MIRACLES

Fifth Review – Lesson 180 – Review of Lessons 169 – 170
God is but Love, and therefore so am I.
1. (169) By grace I live. By grace I am released.
2. (170) There is no cruelty in God and none in me.

365 DAYS OF MIRACLES

Lesson 181
I trust my brothers, who are one with me.

365 DAYS OF MIRACLES

Lesson 182
I will be still an instant and go home.

365 DAYS OF MIRACLES

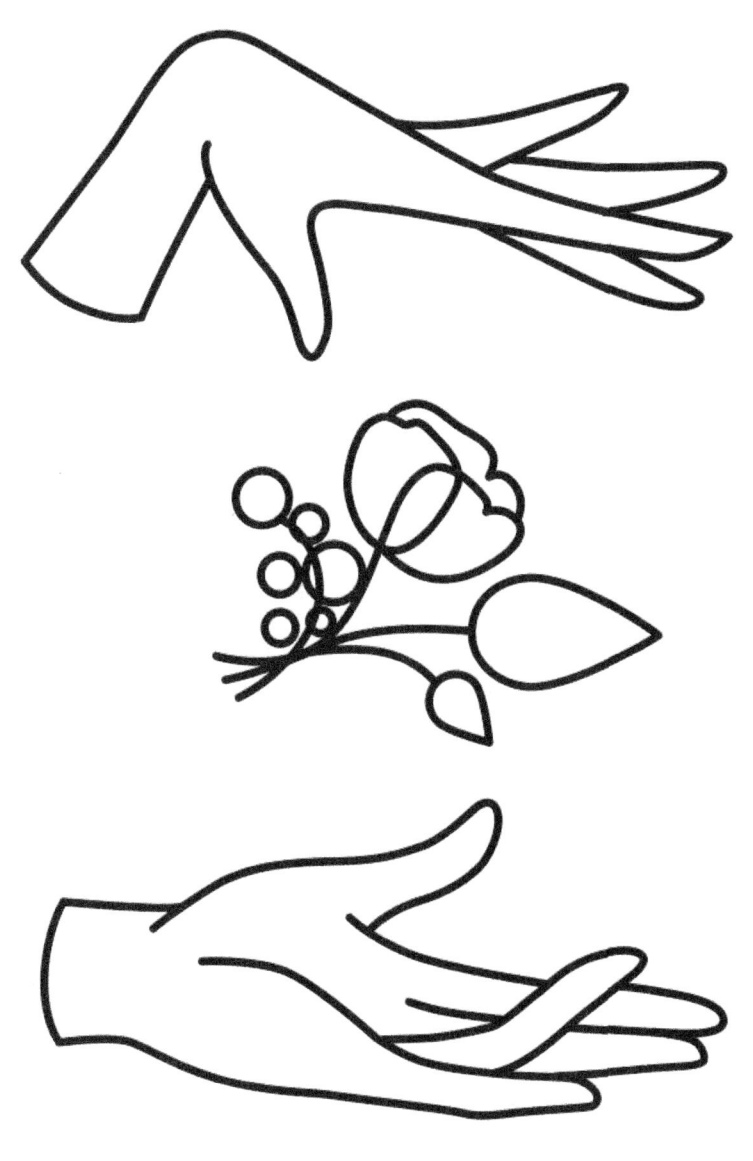

Lesson 183
I call upon God's Name and on my own.

365 DAYS OF MIRACLES

Lesson 184
The Name of God is my inheritance.

Lesson 185
I want the peace of God.

365 DAYS OF MIRACLES

Lesson 186
Salvation of the world depends on me.

365 DAYS OF MIRACLES

Lesson 187
I bless the world because I bless myself.

Lesson 188
The peace of God is shining in me now.

Lesson 189
I feel the Love of God within me now.

365 DAYS OF MIRACLES

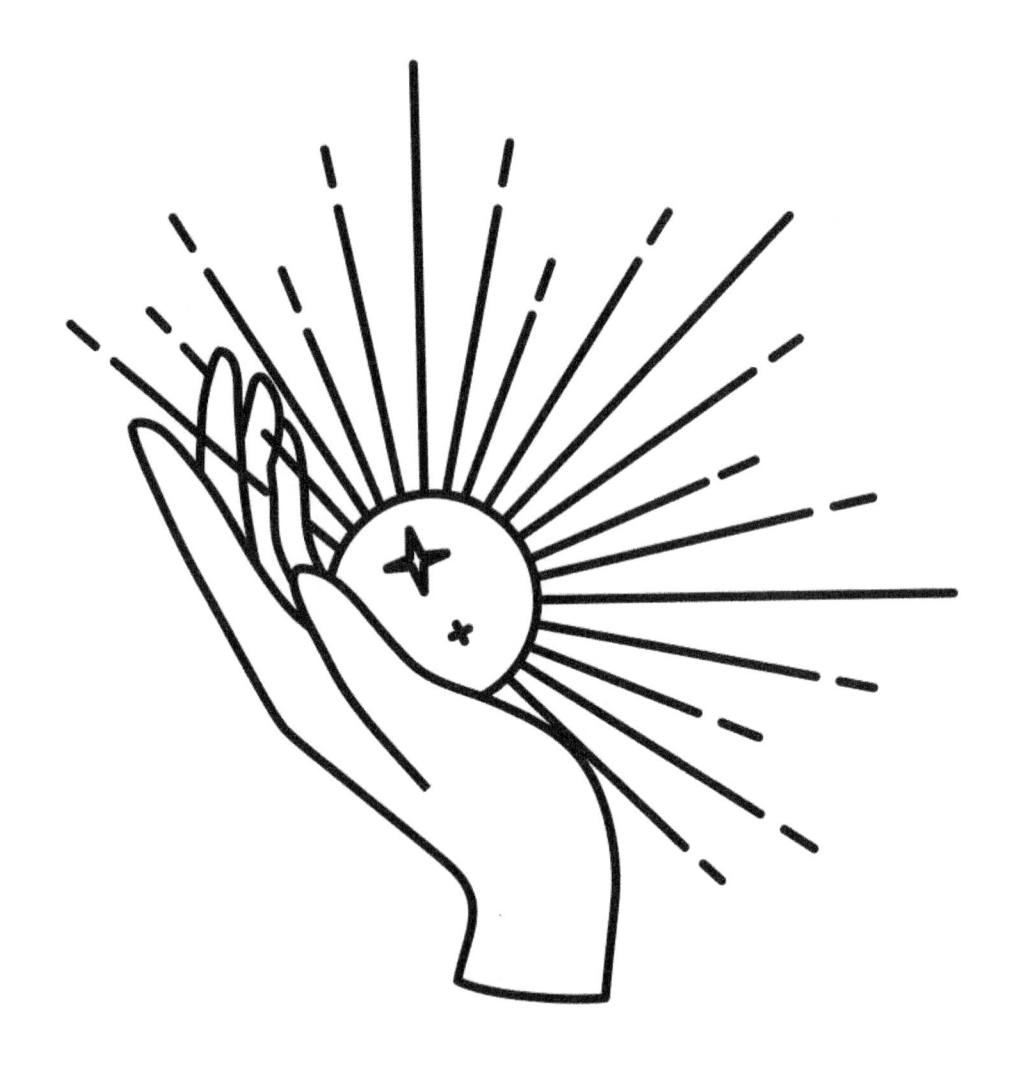

Lesson 190
I choose the joy of God instead of pain.

Lesson 191
I am the holy Son of God Himself.

365 DAYS OF MIRACLES

Lesson 192
I have a function God would have me fill.

Lesson 193
All things are lessons God would have me learn

365 DAYS OF MIRACLES

Lesson 194
I place the future in the Hands of God

365 DAYS OF MIRACLES

Lesson 195
Love is the way I walk in gratitude.

365 DAYS OF MIRACLES

Lesson 196
It can be but myself I crucify

365 DAYS OF MIRACLES

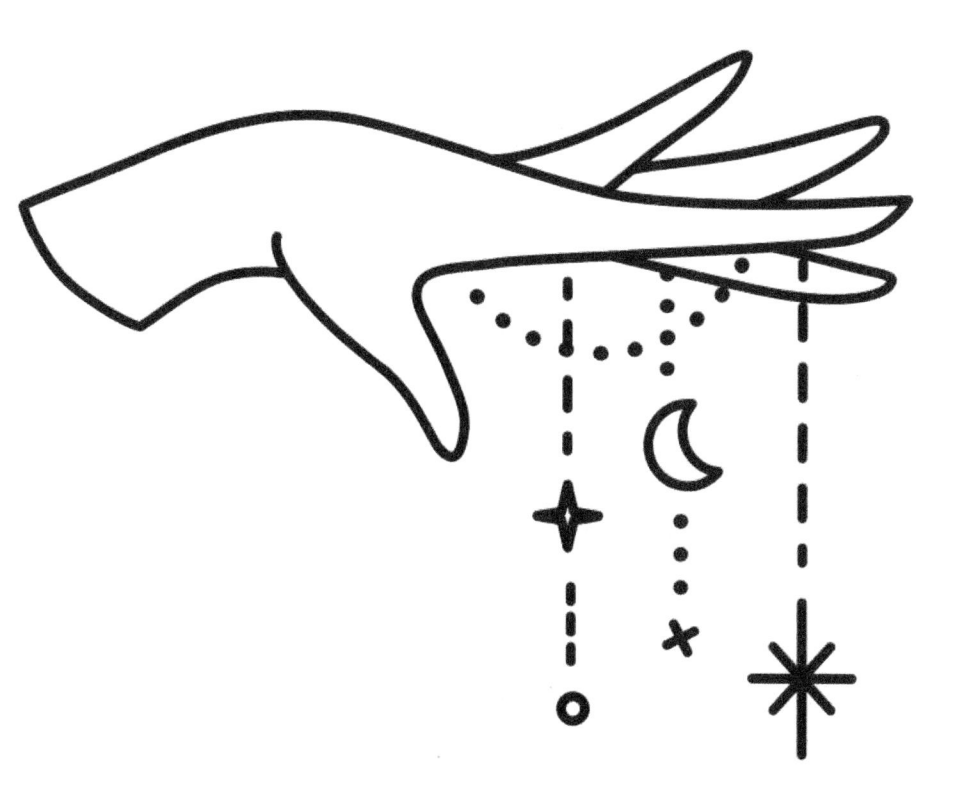

Lesson 197
It can be but my gratitude I earn.

365 DAYS OF MIRACLES

Lesson 198
Only my condemnation injures me.

365 DAYS OF MIRACLES

Lesson 199
I am not a body, I am free.

Lesson 200
There is no peace except the peace of God.

Sixth Review - Lesson 201
I am not a body. I am free.
For I am still as God created me.
1. (181) I trust my brothers, who are one with me.

Sixth Review – Lesson 202
I am not a body. I am free.
For I am still as God created me.
1. (182) I will be still an instant and go home.

Sixth Review – Lesson 203
I am not a body. I am free.
For I am still as God created me.
1. (183) I call upon God's Name and on my own.

365 DAYS OF MIRACLES

Sixth Review – Lesson 204
I am not a body. I am free.
For I am still as God created me.
1. (184) The Name of God is my inheritance.

365 DAYS OF MIRACLES

Sixth Review – Lesson 205
I am not a body. I am free.
For I am still as God created me.
1. (185) I want the peace of God.

365 DAYS OF MIRACLES

Sixth Review – Lesson 206
I am not a body. I am free.
For I am still as God created me.
1. (186) Salvation of the world depends on me.

Sixth Review – Lesson 207
I am not a body. I am free.
For I am still as God created me.
1. (187) I bless the world because I bless myself.

365 DAYS OF MIRACLES

Sixth Review – Lesson 208
I am not a body. I am free.
For I am still as God created me.
1. (188) The peace of God is shining in me now.

365 DAYS OF MIRACLES

Sixth Review – Lesson 209
I am not a body. I am free.
For I am still as God created me.
1. (189) I feel the Love of God within me now.

365 DAYS OF MIRACLES

Sixth Review – Lesson 210
I am not a body. I am free.
For I am still as God created me.
1. (190) I choose the joy of God instead of pain.

365 DAYS OF MIRACLES

Sixth Review - Lesson 211
I am not a body. I am free.
For I am still as God created me.
1. (191) I am the holy Son of God Himself.

Sixth Review - Lesson 212
I am not a body. I am free.
For I am still as God created me.
1. (192) I have a function God would have me fill.

Sixth Review – Lesson 213
I am not a body. I am free.
For I am still as God created me.
1. (193) All things are lessons God would have me learn.

365 DAYS OF MIRACLES

Sixth Review - Lesson 214
I am not a body. I am free.
For I am still as God created me.
1. (194) I place the future in the Hands of God.

365 DAYS OF MIRACLES

Sixth Review - Lesson 215
I am not a body. I am free.
For I am still as God created me.
1. (195) Love is the way I walk in gratitude.

365 DAYS OF MIRACLES

Sixth Review – Lesson 216
I am not a body. I am free.
For I am still as God created me.
1. (196) It can be but myself I crucify.

365 DAYS OF MIRACLES

Sixth Review - Lesson 217
I am not a body. I am free.
For I am still as God created me.
1. (197) It can be but my gratitude I earn.

Sixth Review – Lesson 218
I am not a body. I am free.
For I am still as God created me.
1. (198) Only my condemnation injures me.

Sixth Review - Lesson 219
I am not a body. I am free.
For I am still as God created me.
1. (199) I am not a body. I am free.

Sixth Review – Lesson 220
I am not a body. I am free.
For I am still as God created me.
1. (200) There is no peace except the peace of God.

Lesson 221
Peace to my mind. Let all my thoughts be still.

Lesson 222
God is with me. I live and move in Him.

Lesson 223
God is my life. I have no life but His.

Lesson 224
God is my Father, and He loves His Son.

Lesson 225
God is my Father, and His Son loves Him.

365 DAYS OF MIRACLES

Lesson 226
My home awaits me. I will hasten there.

Lesson 227
This is my holy instant of release.

Lesson 228
God has condemned me not. No more do I.

Lesson 229
Love, which created me, is what I am.

365 DAYS OF MIRACLES

Lesson 230
Now will I seek and find the peace of God.

365 DAYS OF MIRACLES

Lesson 231
Father, I will but to remember You.

365 DAYS OF MIRACLES

Lesson 232
Be in my mind, my Father, through the day.

365 DAYS OF MIRACLES

Lesson 233
I give my life to God to guide today.

365 DAYS OF MIRACLES

Lesson 234
Father, today I am Your Son again.

Lesson 235
God in His mercy wills that I be saved.

365 DAYS OF MIRACLES

Lesson 236
I rule my mind, which I alone must rule.

Lesson 237
Now would I be as God created me.

365 DAYS OF MIRACLES

Lesson 238
On my decision all salvation rests.

365 DAYS OF MIRACLES

Lesson 239
The glory of my Father is my own.

365 DAYS OF MIRACLES

Lesson 240
Fear is not justified in any form.

Lesson 241
This holy instant is salvation come.

Lesson 242
This day is God's. It is my gift to Him.

Lesson 243
Today I will judge nothing that occurs.

Lesson 244
I am in danger nowhere in the world.

Lesson 245
Your peace is with me, Father. I am safe.

365 DAYS OF MIRACLES

Lesson 246
To love my Father is to love His Son.

365 DAYS OF MIRACLES

Lesson 247
Without forgiveness I will still be blind.

Lesson 248
Whatever suffers is not part of me.

Lesson 249
Forgiveness ends all suffering and loss.

365 DAYS OF MIRACLES

Lesson 250
Let me not see myself as limited.

Lesson 251
I am in need of nothing but the truth.

Lesson 252
The Son of God is my Identity.

Lesson 253
My Self is ruler of the universe.

365 DAYS OF MIRACLES

Lesson 254
Let every voice but God's be still in me.

365 DAYS OF MIRACLES

Lesson 255
This day I choose to spend in perfect peace.

365 DAYS OF MIRACLES

Lesson 256
God is the only goal I have today.

365 DAYS OF MIRACLES

Lesson 257
Let me remember what my purpose is.

365 DAYS OF MIRACLES

Lesson 258
Let me remember that my goal is God.

Lesson 259
Let me remember that there is no sin.

365 DAYS OF MIRACLES

Lesson 260
Let me remember God created me.

365 DAYS OF MIRACLES

Lesson 261
God is my refuge and security.

Lesson 262
Let me perceive no differences today.

Lesson 263
My holy vision sees all things as pure.

365 DAYS OF MIRACLES

Lesson 264
I am surrounded by the Love of God.

365 DAYS OF MIRACLES

Lesson 265
Creation's gentleness is all I see.

365 DAYS OF MIRACLES

Lesson 266
My holy Self abides in you, God's Son.

Lesson 267
My heart is beating in the peace of God.

365 DAYS OF MIRACLES

Lesson 268
Let all things be exactly as they are.

Lesson 269
My sight goes forth to look upon Christ's face.

365 DAYS OF MIRACLES

Lesson 270
I will not use the body's eyes today.

365 DAYS OF MIRACLES

Lesson 271
Christ's is the vision I will use today.

365 DAYS OF MIRACLES

Lesson 272
How can illusions satisfy God's Son?

Lesson 273
The stillness of the peace of God is mine.

Lesson 274
Today belongs to love. Let me not fear.

Lesson 275
God's healing Voice protects all things today.

365 DAYS OF MIRACLES

Lesson 276
The Word of God is given me to speak.

Lesson 277
Let me not bind Your Son with laws I made.

365 DAYS OF MIRACLES

Lesson 278
If I am bound, my Father is not free.

Lesson 279
Creation's freedom promises my own.

Lesson 280
What limits can I lay upon God's Son?

Lesson 281
I can be hurt by nothing but my thoughts.

Lesson 282
I will not be afraid of love today.

Lesson 283
My true Identity abides in You.

365 DAYS OF MIRACLES

Lesson 284
I can elect to change all thoughts that hurt.

Lesson 285
My holiness shines bright and clear today.

365 DAYS OF MIRACLES

Lesson 286
The hush of Heaven holds my heart today.

Lesson 287
You are my goal, my Father. Only You.

365 DAYS OF MIRACLES

Lesson 288
Let me forget my brother's past today.

365 DAYS OF MIRACLES

Lesson 289
The past is over. It can touch me not.

365 DAYS OF MIRACLES

Lesson 290
My present happiness is all I see.

Lesson 291
This is a day of stillness and of peace.

365 DAYS OF MIRACLES

Lesson 292
A happy outcome to all things is sure.

Lesson 293
All fear is past and only love is here.

365 DAYS OF MIRACLES

Lesson 294
My body is a wholly neutral thing.

365 DAYS OF MIRACLES

Lesson 295
The Holy Spirit looks through me today.

365 DAYS OF MIRACLES

BLAH BLAH BLAH

Lesson 296
The Holy Spirit speaks through me today.

Lesson 297
Forgiveness is the only gift I give.

365 DAYS OF MIRACLES

Lesson 298
I love You, Father, and I love Your Son.

Lesson 299
Eternal holiness abides in me.

365 DAYS OF MIRACLES

Lesson 300
Only an instant does this world endure.

365 DAYS OF MIRACLES

Lesson 301
And God Himself shall wipe away all tears.

Lesson 302
Where darkness was I look upon the light.

Lesson 303
The holy Christ is born in me today.

365 Days of Miracles

Lesson 304
Let not my world obscure the sight of Christ.

Lesson 305
There is a peace that Christ bestows on us.

365 DAYS OF MIRACLES

Lesson 306
The gift of Christ is all I seek today.

365 DAYS OF MIRACLES

Lesson 307
Conflicting wishes cannot be my will.

Lesson 308
This instant is the only time there is.

365 DAYS OF MIRACLES

Lesson 309
I will not fear to look within today.

365 DAYS OF MIRACLES

I love me

Lesson 310
In fearlessness and love I spend today.

Lesson 311
I judge all things as I would have them be.

365 DAYS OF MIRACLES

Lesson 312
I see all things as I would have them be.

365 DAYS OF MIRACLES

Lesson 313
Now let a new perception come to me.

365 DAYS OF MIRACLES

Lesson 314
I seek a future different from the past.

Lesson 315
All gifts my brothers give belong to me.

365 DAYS OF MIRACLES

Lesson 316
All gifts I give my brothers are my own.

365 DAYS OF MIRACLES

Lesson 317
I follow in the way appointed me.

Lesson 318
In me salvation's means and end are one.

365 DAYS OF MIRACLES

Lesson 319
I came for the salvation of the world.

365 DAYS OF MIRACLES

Lesson 320
My Father gives all power unto me.

Lesson 321
Father, my freedom is in You alone.

365 DAYS OF MIRACLES

Lesson 322
I can give up but what was never real.

365 DAYS OF MIRACLES

Lesson 323
I gladly make the "sacrifice" of fear.

Lesson 324
I merely follow, for I would not lead.

365 DAYS OF MIRACLES

Lesson 325
All things I think I see reflect ideas.

Lesson 326
I am forever an Effect of God.

Lesson 327
I need but call and You will answer me.

365 DAYS OF MIRACLES

Lesson 328
I choose the second place to gain the first.

365 DAYS OF MIRACLES

Lesson 329
I have already chosen what You will.

365 DAYS OF MIRACLES

Lesson 330
I will not hurt myself again today.

365 DAYS OF MIRACLES

Lesson 331
There is no conflict, for my will is Yours.

365 DAYS OF MIRACLES

Lesson 332
Fear binds the world. Forgiveness sets it free.

365 DAYS OF MIRACLES

Lesson 333
Forgiveness ends the dream of conflict here.

365 DAYS OF MIRACLES

Lesson 334
Today I claim the gifts forgiveness gives.

Lesson 335
I choose to see my brother's sinlessness.

Lesson 336
Forgiveness lets me know that minds are joined.

365 DAYS OF MIRACLES

Lesson 337
My sinlessness protects me from all harm.

365 DAYS OF MIRACLES

Lesson 338
I am affected only by my thoughts.

365 DAYS OF MIRACLES

Lesson 339
I will receive whatever I request.

365 DAYS OF MIRACLES

Lesson 340
I can be free of suffering today.

Lesson 341
I can attack but my own sinlessness,
And it is only that which keeps me safe.

365 DAYS OF MIRACLES

Lesson 342
I let forgiveness rest upon all things,
For thus forgiveness will be given me.

Lesson 343
I am not asked to make a sacrifice
To find the mercy and the peace of God.

365 DAYS OF MIRACLES

Lesson 344
Today I learn the law of love; that what
I give my brother is my gift to me.

Lesson 345
I offer only miracles today,
For I would have them be returned to me.

Lesson 346
Today the peace of God envelops me,
And I forget all things except His Love.

365 DAYS OF MIRACLES

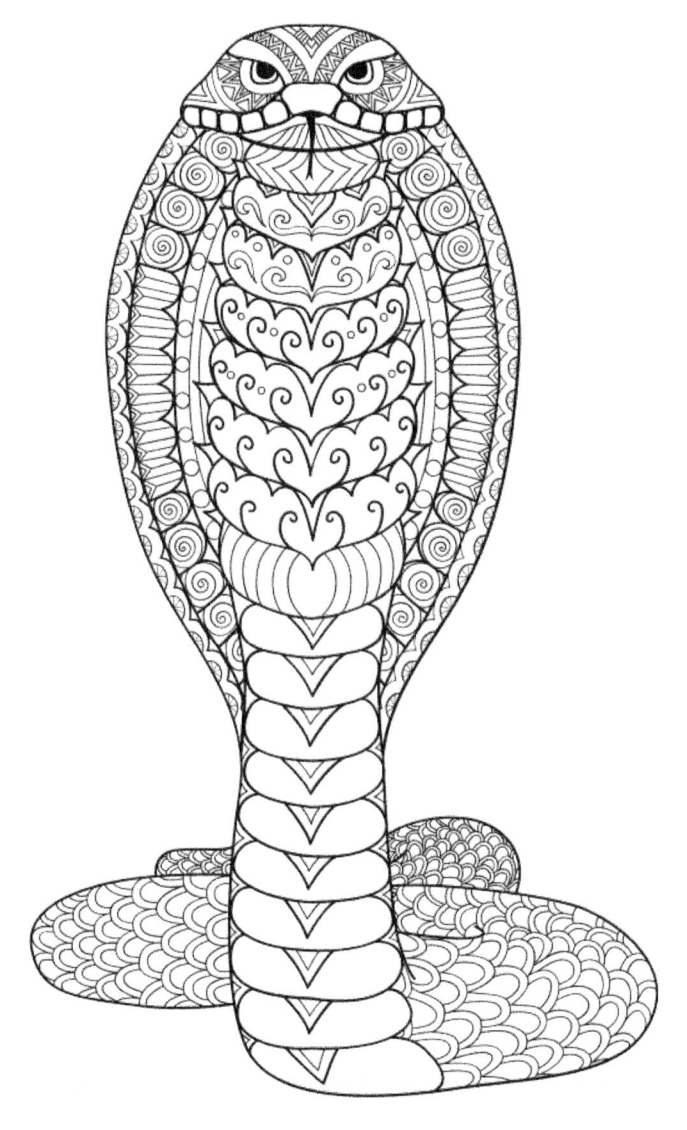

Lesson 347
Anger must come from judgment. Judgment is
The weapon I would use against myself,
To keep the miracle away from me.

365 DAYS OF MIRACLES

Lesson 348
I have no cause for anger or for fear,
For You surround me. And in every need
That I perceive, Your grace suffices me.

Lesson 349
Today I let Christ's vision look upon
All things for me and judge them not, but give
Each one a miracle of love instead.

365 DAYS OF MIRACLES

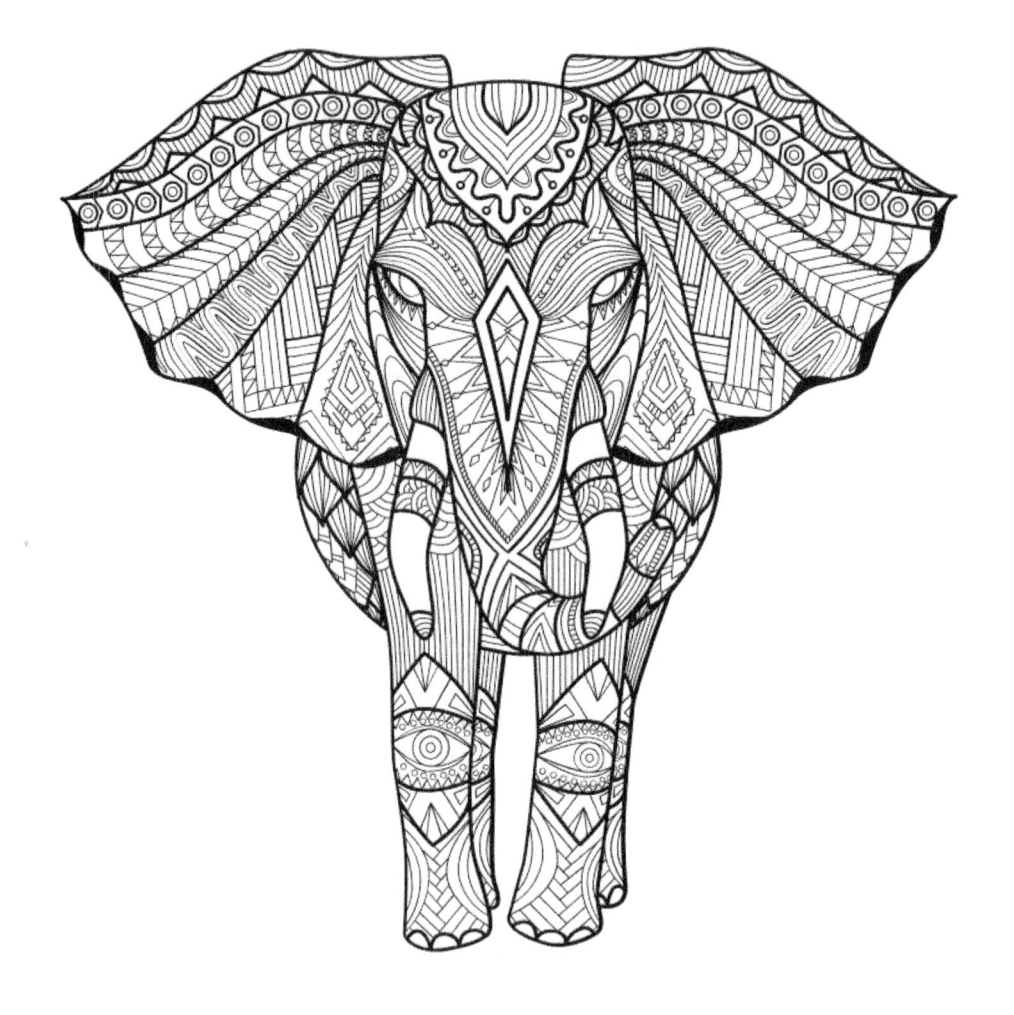

Lesson 350
Miracles mirror God's eternal Love.
To offer them is to remember Him,
And through His memory to save the world.

Lesson 351
My sinless brother is my guide to peace.
My sinful brother is my guide to pain.
And which I choose to see I will behold.

Lesson 352
Judgment and love are opposites. From one come all the sorrows of the world. But from the other comes the peace of God Himself.

Lesson 353
My eyes, my tongue, my hands, my feet today have but one purpose; to be given Christ to use to bless the world with miracles.

Lesson 354
We stand together, Christ and I, in peace and certainty of purpose. And in Him is His Creator, as He is in me.

Lesson 355

There is no end to all the peace and joy, and all the miracles that I will give, when I accept God's Word. Why not today?

365 DAYS OF MIRACLES

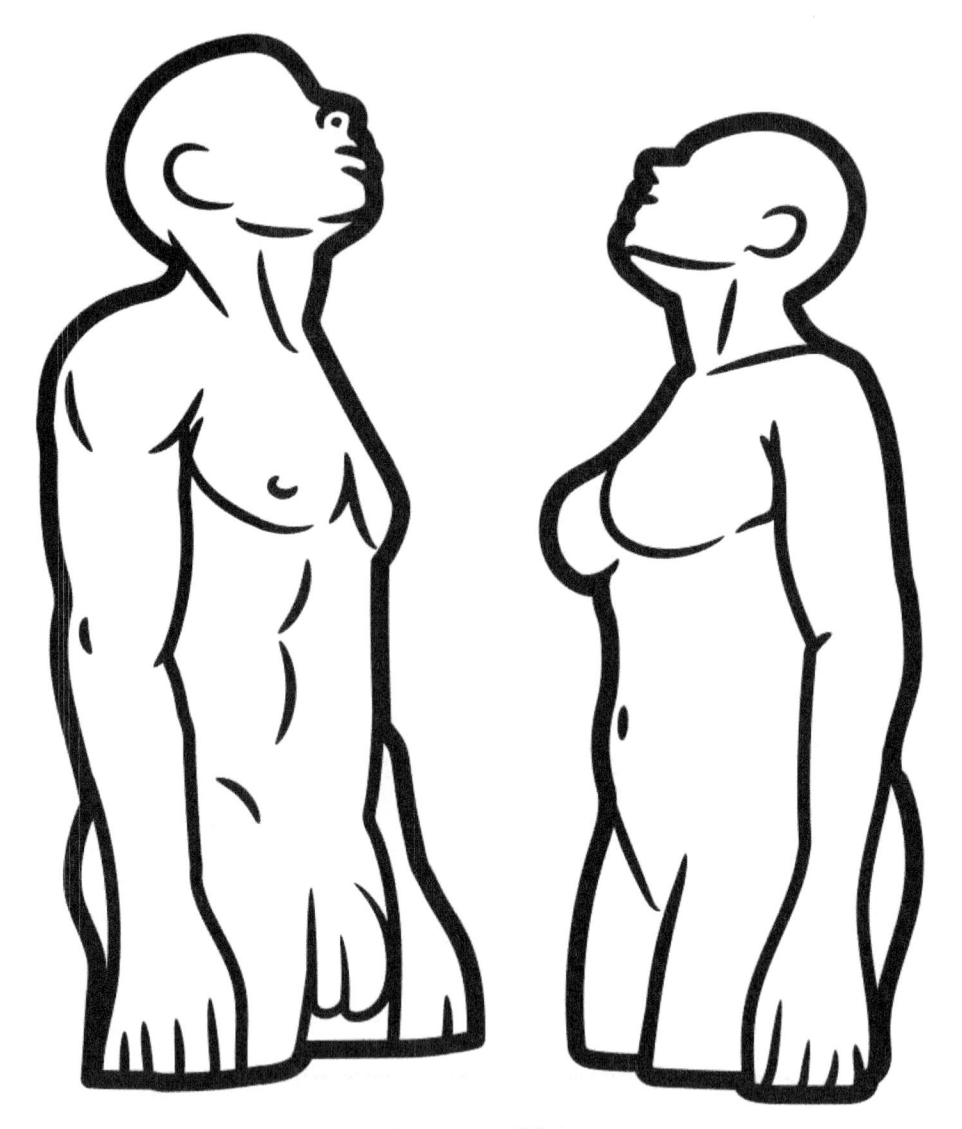

Lesson 356
Sickness is but another name for sin.
Healing is but another name for God.
The miracle is thus a call to Him.

Lesson 357
Truth answers every call we make to God, responding first with miracles, and then returning unto us to be itself.

Lesson 358
No call to God can be unheard nor left unanswered. And of this I can be sure; His answer is the one I really want.

365 DAYS OF MIRACLES

Lesson 359
God's answer is some form of peace. All pain is healed; all misery replaced with joy. All prison doors are opened. And all sin is understood as merely a mistake.

365 DAYS OF MIRACLES

Lesson 360
Peace be to me, the holy Son of God.
Peace to my brother, who is one with me.
Let all the world be blessed with peace through us.

365 DAYS OF MIRACLES

Final Lessons 361-365
This holy instant would I give to You.
Be You in charge. For I would follow You, certain that Your direction gives me peace.

Thank You

for choosing us
throughout this year.

◎ @PSIC.CAROLINALASSOR

Printed in Great Britain
by Amazon